JIM ARNOSKY

CREEP and FLUTTER

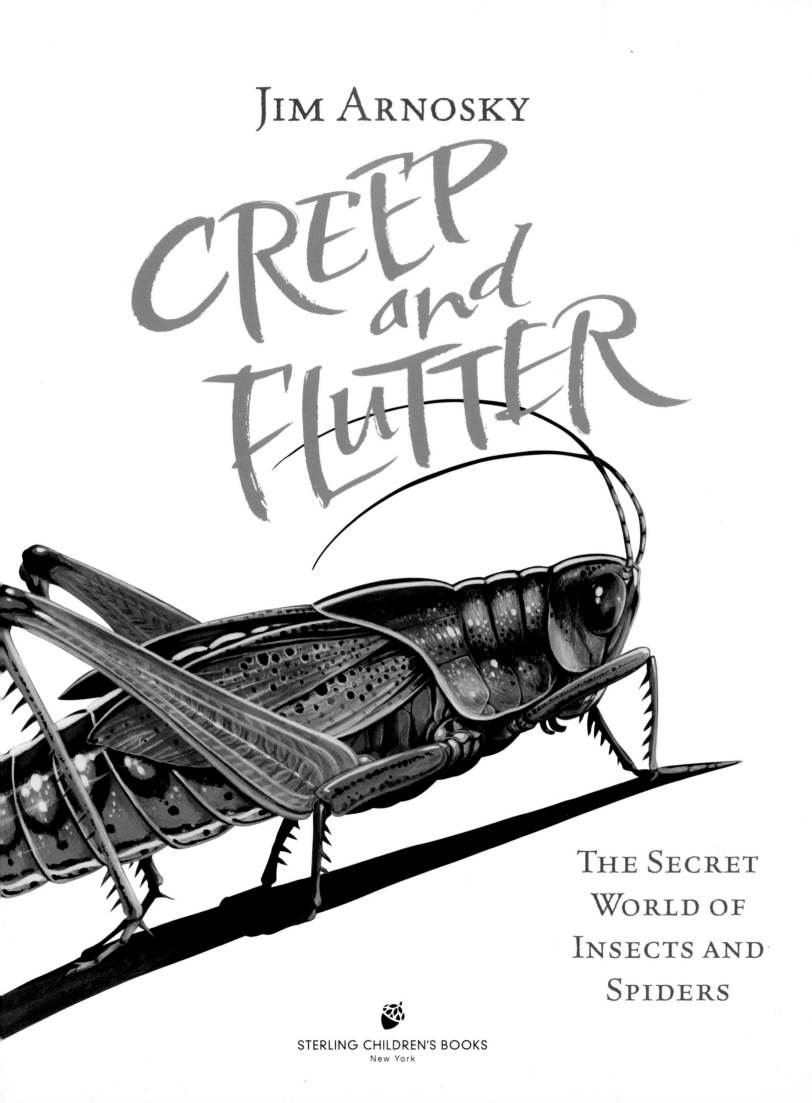

THE SECRET
WORLD OF
INSECTS AND
SPIDERS

STERLING CHILDREN'S BOOKS
New York

To Franck and Ulla Britt

STERLING CHILDREN'S BOOKS
New York

An Imprint of Sterling Publishing
387 Park Avenue South
New York, NY 10016

STERLING CHILDREN'S BOOKS and the distinctive Sterling
Children's Books logo are trademarks of Sterling Publishing Co., Inc.

© 2012 by Jim Arnosky
Display lettering created by Georgia Deaver
Designed by Jen Browning
The artwork for this book was prepared using pencil and acrylic paints.

ISBN 978-1-4027-7766-0 (hardcover)

Library of Congress Cataloging-in-Publication Data

Arnosky, Jim.
  Creep and flutter : the secret world of insects and spiders / by Jim Arnosky.
    p. cm.
  ISBN 978-1-4027-7766-0
  1. Insects--Juvenile literature. 2. Spiders--Juvenile literature. I. Title.
  QL467.2.A774 2011
  595.7--dc22

                            2011004626

Distributed in Canada by Sterling Publishing
c/o Canadian Manda Group, 165 Dufferin Street
Toronto, Ontario, Canada M6K 3H6
Distributed in the United Kingdom by GMC Distribution Services
Castle Place, 166 High Street, Lewes, East Sussex, England BN7 1XU
Distributed in Australia by Capricorn Link (Australia) Pty. Ltd.
P.O. Box 704, Windsor, NSW 2756, Australia

For information about custom editions, special sales, and premium and
corporate purchases, please contact Sterling Special Sales at 800-805-5489 or
specialsales@sterlingpublishing.com.

Manufactured in China

Lot #:
10 9 8 7 6 5 4 3 2 1
12/11

www.sterlingpublishing.com/kids

CONTENTS

SPOTTED TUSSOCK MOTH CATERPILLAR

Introduction

One day I hiked up to the ancient granite quarry behind our farm. Glancing down at the pebbled ground, I spotted the silent movement of a large yellow-and-black caterpillar that I could not identify. Kneeling to get closer, I took out my notepad and sketched the caterpillar life-size. That quick outdoor sketch and my determination to learn the identity of the beautiful creature I had seen began a most wonderful adventure into the secret world of insects.

Insects and their close relatives, spiders, belong to a huge group of animals known as arthropods. Arthropod means "jointed foot." Scorpions, crabs, and lobsters are also arthropods. Of all the animals, arthropods are the most numerous. Insects alone outnumber all the other creatures on Earth combined.

In this book I had to make difficult choices about which types of insects and spiders to show you. You will see that on most pages I have worked larger than lifesize, to allow you to see the intricate nature of these creatures. The actual size of each is shown as a silhouette. I chose a select few to showcase their splendid variety—all the hum and buzz, as well as their beauty. Enough, I hope, to get you wondering about the millions of insects and spiders already known in our world, and the millions more that may yet be discovered.

Jim Arnosky

white spikes Yellow middle Black spots

Caterpillar life size

Milkweed Bug

Crab Spider

Dragonfly nymphs are called naiads (pronounced NIGH-ads). They live on after mating and feed on smaller insects. When you see a dragonfly hovering or zipping by, it is hunting for prey. Different members of the dragonfly family can be identified by shape.

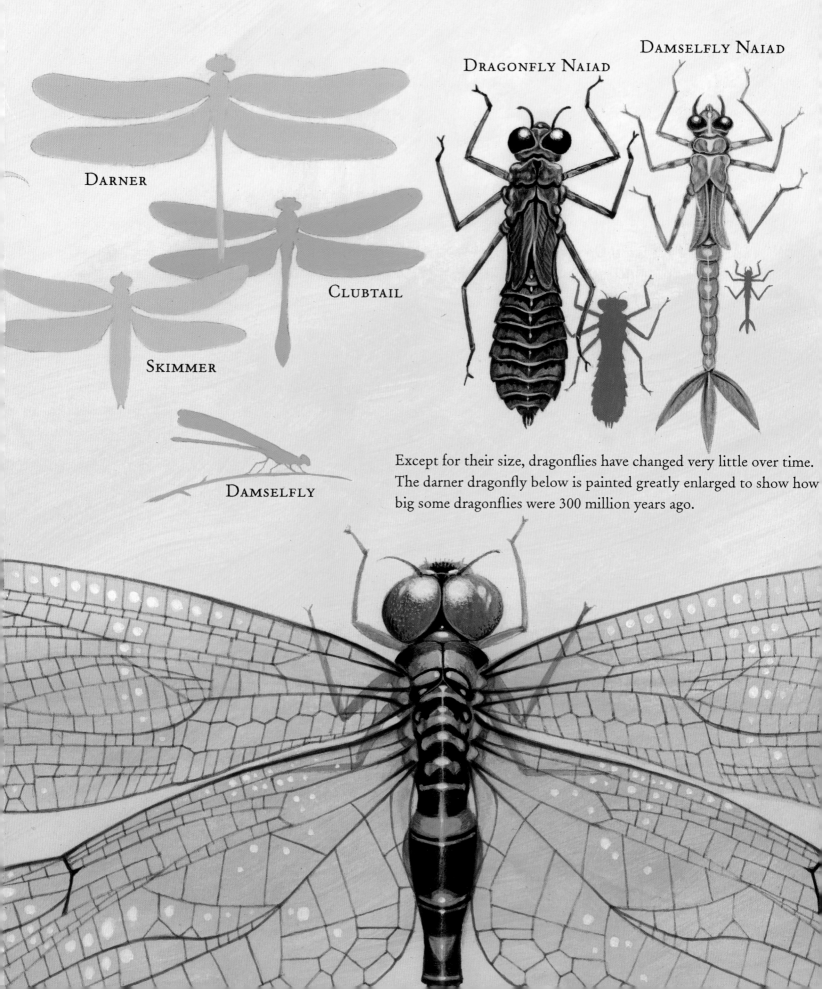

DARNER

CLUBTAIL

SKIMMER

DAMSELFLY

DRAGONFLY NAIAD

DAMSELFLY NAIAD

Except for their size, dragonflies have changed very little over time. The darner dragonfly below is painted greatly enlarged to show how big some dragonflies were 300 million years ago.

SUPERSIZED MAYFLIES, DRAGONFLIES, STONEFLIES, AND CADDISFLIES

There are small, medium, and large species of mayfly. (Silhouettes show actual size.)

The largest mayflies live in still waters, where their nymphs (larvae) can burrow into the soft and silty bottom.

Most medium-sized mayflies (above) and small mayflies (below) are found in fast-moving streams.

Chitin (pronounced KY-tin) is the tough covering that forms the outer skeleton of insects, arachnids, and crustaceans. The flat, chitin-covered bodies of nymphs protect them as they search for food between and beneath heavy and often shifting stream boulders.

PARTS OF A MAYFLY NYMPH
(The nymphs of all aquatic insects are similar.)

antenna

leg

mouth

eye

thorax

abdomen

gills

tails

(actual size)

A network of veins adds strength and flexibility to insect wings.

7

RAINBOW TROUT AND GIANT MAYFLIES

Mayflies, Dragonflies, Stoneflies, and Caddisflies

Mayfly

I know a secret place where the rare *Hexagenia limbata*—the largest of all mayfly species—lives. And every year around the middle of June, something truly spectacular happens. Thousands of Hexagenia nymphs, having lived all their lives underwater, suddenly swim to the surface, shed their nymphal skins, and emerge as winged mayflies. Their flight fills the air with motion, triggering a leaping and splashing feeding frenzy among the pond's rainbow trout.

Stonefly

Although you may see many insects in and around water, true aquatic insects live much of their lives underwater in the form of nymphs (larvae) before swimming to the surface. Four aquatic insects known the world over are the mayfly, dragonfly, stonefly, and caddisfly. These insects, so familiar to us in their terrestrial form, begin life as microscopic eggs deposited in water by their airborne mothers. The eggs hatch into nymphs, or in the case of caddisflies, they hatch into worm-like larvae and immediately begin feeding on algae and organic debris.

Caddisfly

The nymphs grow quickly, shedding their skins each time they increase in size. Then they swim to the surface, shed their last nymphal skin, and take to the air as winged adults. The males and females mate in flight. The females deposit their eggs in the water, and the cycle continues.

Dragonfly

Winged Fly

Egg

Nymph

Emerging Nymph

By itself, the soft-bodied, slow-moving caddisworm has little protection against the rough environment of a rushing stream or against predators such as dragonfly nymphs and fish. To survive, a caddisworm constructs a sturdy case of natural materials, all held together by a special glue-like secretion it makes. One end of the case is left open for the worm to reach out and gather its microscopic food.

The design and construction of caddisworm cases vary with the species. Here are some of the different types of caddisworm cases I have found. Seen up close, each is a marvel of design and a tiny worm work-of-art.

Caddisworm case of sticks and leaf parts (my favorite!)

Caddisworm case of fine pebbles

Caddisworm case of coarse pebbles

Caddisworm case of grains of sand

Caddisworm case of leaf strips, each uniformly cut by the worm

Stoneflies remind me of ancient warriors in full armor. Because of their large size and extremely slow flight, adult stoneflies can be easily spotted and kept in sight for a long while. In the water, a stonefly nymph's big body, large limbs, and chitin plates marked with light-colored swirls makes it unmistakable.

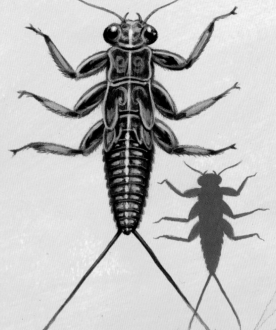

STONEFLY NYMPH

Look for shed stonefly nymph skins on dry stream boulders. They are amazingly durable and can be collected intact.

When their time comes to emerge, stonefly nymphs crawl in groups out of the water and onto dry rocks. Their nymphal skin cracks open and the winged flies crawl out and fly away.

The life cycle of a caddisfly consists of an egg, worm (larva), pupa, and winged adult. An emergence of caddisflies rivals that of the *Hexagenia Limbata* mayfly in spectacular numbers.

Winged adult

Caddisfly at rest

CADDISWORM

A caddisworm changes to a form called a pupa, where it undergoes metamorphosis before emerging as a winged adult.

Pupa

SUPERSIZED BEETLES
AND TRUE BUGS

COTTONWOOD BORER
(5x actual size)

TIGER BEETLE
(10x actual size)

LIGHTNING BEETLE
(firefly) (15x actual size)

MALAYSIAN STAG
BEETLE (actual size)

Beetles and Bugs

A third of all insects are beetles. Beetles are distinguished from all other insects by the two shell-like forewings that lie side by side on the beetle's back when it isn't in flight. These tough, flightless forewings, together called the elytra, cover the beetle's more delicate flight wings. We call some beetles "bugs," but "lightning bugs" and "ladybugs" are actually beetles, not bugs. True bugs do not have elytra covering their flight wings. True bugs have semi-transparent forewings, which do not lie side by side but overlap on the bug's back when it is not in flight.

One winter evening, I was sitting near the woodstove when a lady beetle flew near, slow and unsteady in the air. The tiny insect crashed into a lampshade and dropped to the floor. It lay on its back and didn't even try to right itself.

I picked the tiny beetle up to look at it closely under my microscope. To the naked eye, the beetle looked perfectly smooth. Under the powerful lens, I saw that the elytra had tiny holes or pores. Under the elytra, the flight wings were folded twice, once inward and once up. Spread out, the flight wings were nearly twice as long as their forewing covers.

Seeing the beetle up close and supersized under the microscope lens was like seeing a beetle for the very first time. It excited me and made me want to supersize some beetles in this book so you might also see beetles anew.

Antennae
Thoracic Shield
Forewings (Elytra)
Legs

Beetle Parts

Elytra

Flight Wings

Beetle Flying

No Overlap

Lightning Bug [A Beetle]

Wings Overlap

Mesquite Bug [A True Bug]

Not all insects are bugs. True bugs are a separate order of insects called Hemiptera, which means "half wings." The true bug's forewings are half opaque (solid in color), half transparent, and lie flat, overlapping one another on the bug's back. The smaller pair of hind wings is used for flying. Young bugs are miniature versions of the adults. From the time they hatch, they use their sharply pointed mouths to puncture, bite, and suck plants and, in some species, animals. Some bugs are predatory. Giant water bugs devour aquatic insects and even eat small fish. The tiny wingless bedbug feeds on human blood.

Cicada nymphs burrow underground and feed on the sap in tree roots. Cicada adults feed on the sap in tree leaves.

CICADA AND YOUNG (Nymph)

BEDBUG

Beetle or bug? Some bugs closely resemble beetles. If you are not sure, look for the overlapping wings of the true bug.

GIANT WATER BUG
(actual size)

COTTON STAINER bug

STINKBUG

WATER BOATMEN

Young beetles, called grubs, look nothing like adult beetles. Some, such as the potato beetle grub, vaguely resemble their adults in coloration.

Beetle grubs and adult beetles eat leaves, stems, roots, grains, wood, wool, and animal fur. Some beetle grubs prey on other insects and on earthworms. And there are beetles that feed on carrion, cleaning every last speck of meat off the bones of dead animals.

Beetles are found around the world in every kind of habitat, from deserts to wetlands, in deep sunless caves, and even underwater. Tough and durable, beetles can adapt to change. Certain species are imported from one continent to another for use in controlling other, more harmful insects that destroy farmers' crops.

LADY BEETLE (ladybug)
(18x actual size)

POTATO BEETLE AND GRUB
(silhouettes show actual size)

LEAF BEETLE

SOLDIER BEETLE

WATER SCAVENGER BEETLE

JAPANESE
BEETLE

Above are the four basic beetle body types.

TIGER SWALLOWTAIL
BUTTERFLY AND CATERPILLAR

LUNA MOTH AND
CATERPILLAR

BLACK SWALLOWTAIL
BUTTERFLY AND CATERPILLAR

MONARCH BUTTERFLY
AND CATERPILLAR

PAINTED LADY BUTTERFLY
AND CATERPILLAR

REGAL MOTH AND
CATERPILLAR

SPOTTED
TUSSOCK
MOTH AND
CATERPILLAR

Caterpillars

We once lived in a woodland that was infested by gypsy moths. There were so many leaf-munching gypsy moth caterpillars crowding the trees in springtime that they would overload the twigs and fall to the ground in great numbers. They covered our roof, our walkway, and our road. Passing cars would actually skid and slide on gooey mashed caterpillars.

One day, a scientist came and asked if he could set up a tent in our woods in order to study the caterpillars. It was through his eyes that I learned to see the caterpillars as interesting and beautiful creatures.

Caterpillars are the young form of moths and butterflies. When they hatch from their eggs they are equipped with sharp cutting and chewing jaws so they can immediately begin feeding on leaves. Caterpillars grow fast, molting (shedding) their confining skin each time they outgrow it.

Their slow movement and habit of feeding out in the open make caterpillars vulnerable to predators. They have only their camouflage coloration, ferocious looking markings, or the presence of stinging bristles to protect them. Some, like the gypsy moth caterpillars, protect themselves by feeding only at night. Other species of moth caterpillars spin silken shelters to hide inside or even to hibernate in over winter.

A caterpillar's final molt produces a pupa. A moth pupa covers itself with a silk cocoon. A butterfly pupa is not covered with silk—it is encased in a smooth, transparent secretion that forms a chrysalis. Inside the chrysalis (also called a cocoon) the change from a pupa to winged adult takes place.

Gypsy Moth

Jointed legs

Pro legs

Queen Butterfly Caterpillar 2 X

LIFESIZED BUTTERFLIES AND MOTHS

Butterflies and moths feed on flower nectar, which they suck through a hollow tubelike mouth part, called the proboscis (pruh-BAHS-kus). When the insect is not feeding, its proboscis is tightly coiled. The black-and-white butterfly (shown in close-up in circle) is probing for nectar deep within a flower, using its proboscis like a long straw.

So far, an estimated 20,000 species of butterfly and 125,000 species of moth have been discovered worldwide. Large moths can be found anywhere from deserts to forests. The largest butterflies are found in rainforests.

THOAS SWALLOWTAIL BUTTERFLY (Southern Texas south to Brazil, Caribbean)

MORPHO
RFLY
America)

PARTS OF A BUTTERFLY

forewing (underside)

hind wing

forewing (top side)

antennae

compound eye

whiskers

proboscis

PAINTED LADY BUTTERFLY (found worldwide) (5x actual size)

thorax

leg

abdomen

fly

y

fly

y

20

WESTERN PYGMY BLUE BUTTERFLY
(Western U.S. and Mexico to Venezuela)

BLUE
BUTT
(South

PARADISE BIRDWING
BUTTERFLY
(Australia
and Asia)

Hairstreak Butte

ZEBRA LONGWING BUTTERFLY
(South Texas, Florida, Caribbean,
South America)

Anglewing Butter

MONARCH BUTTERFLY
(Americas, Australia, Europe)

Daggerwing Butter

ZEBRA
SWALLOWTAIL
BUTTERFLY
(North America)

Leafwing Butterf

19   Longwings, swallowtails, hairstreaks, anglewings, daggerwings, and leafwings are groups
of butterflies that can be recognized by their unique shapes.

TIGER SWALLOWTAIL, SUPERSIZED

Wing scales magnified.

Butterflies and Moths

Butterflies and moths make up an order of insects called Lepidoptera, which means "scaled wings." The colors and patterns on a butterfly's or moth's wings are created by microscopic scales covering the transparent wing. All together the scales appear powdery. When you hold a butterfly and some of its color rubs off, that powdery color on your fingers is actually hundreds of individual scales.

Butterflies and moths, though similar, are different in some obvious ways. Moths have much wider bodies than butterflies. Moth antennae are usually short and feathery. Butterfly antennae are long and thin. Moth and butterfly wings are different too. A moth rests with its wings flat on its back. A butterfly rests with its wings held upright. Moths are almost all night fliers. Butterflies are not.

Butterfly at rest.

Moth at rest.

All Lepidoptera begin life in the egg and hatch into caterpillars that feed voraciously on vegetation. Caterpillars grow quickly. When a caterpillar reaches its full size, it turns into a pupa and, eventually, into a winged adult. The process of a caterpillar becoming a moth (or a butterfly) is called metamorphosis and takes about two weeks.

I once discovered a chrysalis just as a fully formed monarch butterfly inside was breaking out. I held very still and watched closely until the magnificent creature freed itself and fluttered away.

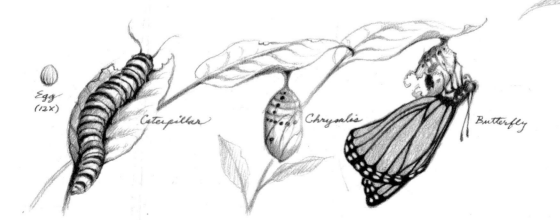

Egg (12x)   *Caterpillar*   *Chrysalis*   *Butterfly*

COMET'S-TAIL
MOTH (India)

SATURNIID MOTH
(Philippines, Brazil)

BIG POPLAR
SPHINX MOTH
(North America)

Some moths are so small they are called micro-moths, no bigger than pygmy blue butterflies. Other moths are huge and are true giants among Lepidoptera. Here are as many as I could fit, shown life-size.

LUNA MOTH (North America)

CECROPIA MOTH
(North America)

At night, butterflies sleep clinging to the underside of leaves, but most moths wake and fly at night.

POLYPHEMUS MOTH
(North America)

BLACK WITCH MOTH
(U.S., Central and South
America, Caribbean)

21

SOUTHERN LUBBER GRASSHOPPER

SUPERSIZED GRASSHOPPERS, KATYDIDS, CRICKETS, AND MANTIDS

The images on the right may look like colorful butterflies, but they are grasshoppers with their hind wings spread.

This blue silhouette shows average actual size.

CAROLINA GRASSHOPPER (sometimes called a Carolina locust)

BLUE-WINGED GRASSHOPPER

ORANGE-WINGED GRASSHOPPER

SULPHUR-WINGED GRASSHOPPER

HORSE LUBBER GRASSHOPPER

There are katydids with long narrow wings and some species with large leaf-shaped wings. The True Katydid (called "true" because it is the species that makes the famous *"katy-did"* sound), has large oval wings.

Katydids primarily feed on the leaves of trees. Crickets burrow down and feed on tree roots.

TRUE KATYDID

FIELD CRICKET

Under the base of the field cricket's forewings are tiny wing scrapers which, when rubbed together, produce a shrill sound.

HONEYBEES AND WILD HIVE

Grasshoppers, Katydids, Crickets, and Mantids

On my first visit to the Florida Everglades, the very first wild animal I saw wasn't an alligator. It wasn't a snake, or even a waterbird. It was a green-and-black grasshopper with a bright yellow stripe down its back. For years I called it my Everglades grasshopper. Its true name is southern lubber and to this day, it remains among the most beautiful wild creatures I've ever encountered.

Grasshoppers, katydids, and crickets belong to an order of insects called Orthoptera, meaning "straight wings." Lubber grasshoppers have short wings. They flutter more than fly. Most grasshoppers have big, powerful wings capable of strong but short flights. Katydids can fly, and spend most of their time in the tops of trees. Crickets have flight wings, but I have never seen a cricket fly, not even to escape capture. Cricket wings are used primarily for producing sound. Crickets, grasshoppers, and katydids rub their wings (not their legs) together to create their song—trilling, chirping, and singing to attract mates or establish territory.

Mantids are distant relatives of grasshoppers. The best known member of the mantid family, the praying mantis, will eat insects, small frogs, salamanders, tiny lizards, and anything else it can seize and hold with its strong, grasping forelegs. A praying mantis will even eat another praying mantis.

straight wings

Forewing

Hind Wing

Katydid

Cricket

Mantis

27

The praying mantis is the T. rex of the insect world. It is native to Europe and was introduced to the United States by gardeners around 1899. Large, silent, and unmoving, the praying mantis waits for food to wander near. Then it pounces, grasping its victim in its strong spiked forelegs while cutting it apart with sharp, scissorlike jaws.

The praying mantis is named for the way it holds its forelegs clasped together, as if in prayer.

26

Bees, Wasps, Ants, and Flies

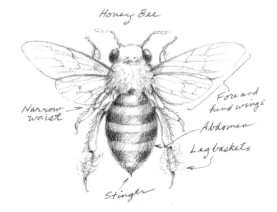

Honey Bee

Narrow waist

Fore and hind wings

Abdomen

Leg baskets

Stinger

I kept bees for years, but I was not a good beekeeper. No matter how quietly I approached, or how much I clouded the air with my bee smoker (a small can that pumped out smoke to calm the bees), I couldn't get past their guards. They would swarm out at me through the smoke and find places in my protective beekeeping clothes where they could get through. I never got away with any of their golden treasure without paying for it in stings.

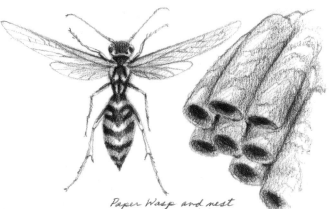

Paper Wasp and nest

Bees, wasps, and ants belong to an order of insects called Hymenoptera, which means "membranous wings." Their four wings are darkened by a network of microscopic veins. There are 108,000 species of Hymenoptera worldwide. All of them begin life in the egg, hatch into larva, and develop from larva to pupa to adult. Hymenoptera are known for the elaborate nests they make. Honeybees create hives, labyrinths of wax honeycomb in which they store honey and raise their young. Bees produce all this from nectar (which they sip from flowers), pollen carried in their leg baskets, and wax secreted from their abdomens.

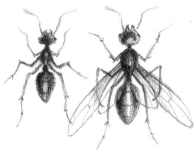

Carpenter Ant and winged queen

Bees, wasps, and ants all have a narrow waist. Flies are sometimes mistaken for bees or wasps, but flies have wider waists and only two wings, instead of four.

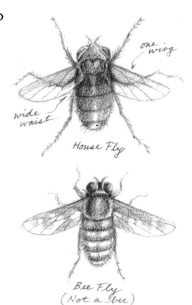

one wing

wide waist

House Fly

Bee Fly
(Not a Bee)

Nursery and food storage cells

Passageways

Entrance

ANTS

Working together, ants can dig a labyrinth of underground tunnels and chambers, moving mountains of sand, soil, and pebbles. A colony can be 8,000 strong with a queen, soldiers, workers, reproductive males, larval young and nurses to care for them.

CORNFIELD ANT
(30x actual size)

TERMITE
(antlike
but not
an ant)

FIRE ANT

CARPENTER ANT

VELVET ANT
(actually an
antlike wasp)

FLIES AND MOSQUITOES

The insect order Diptera includes a wide variety of insects, from diminutive mosquitoes to big, burly horse flies. All have just two wings. And while we consider many of these insects to be pests, they are as beneficial as they are annoying. Mosquitoes and flies are food for fish, birds, amphibians, reptiles, and mammals. And their persistent biting can force a whole herd of cattle or elk to move on, preventing them from overgrazing any one spot.

MOSQUITO

BLACK FLY

CRANE FLY

DEER FLY

GOLDEN-SILK SPIDER

SUPERSIZED BEES, WASPS, ANTS, AND FLIES

YELLOW BUMBLEBEE

Hymenoptera live in highly organized societies. Honeybees have the most complex society with one queen as the mother of the entire hive, drones (males) whose only purpose is for reproduction, and an army of workers (females) who gather nectar and pollen, build wax comb, produce honey, and care for the young.

As a bee moves from flower to flower gathering pollen in its leg baskets, some of the pollen rubs off. This transfers pollen from flower to flower, fertilizing the plants so that they may produce fruits and vegetables.

Wasps also feed on pollen and nectar and are important in the fertilization of plants, but not to the extent honeybees are. Many female wasps can sting and will do so to defend their nests. The nests that wasps build to brood their young are made of either mud or paper, depending on the species.

MUD-DAUBER NEST
(actual size)

YELLOWJACKET
Yellowjackets nest underground.

MUD-DAUBER WASP

BALD-FACED HORNET NEST
(actual size)

BALD-FACED HORNET

29

Spiders and Other Arachnids

I was following a sandy seaside trail when I accidentally walked into the huge web of a golden-silk spider, the first I had ever seen. The golden-silk is a large, rare, stunningly beautiful orb-weaver spider that stretches its web across the paths and trails of forests and swamps in the southern United States. The huge web is always angled vertically in order to trap flying insects. Evidently, flying insects follow the same trails we do, because the sandy footpath was blocked again and again by the spiders' giant wheel-shaped webs.

Spiders are not insects. They are arachnids, along with scorpions, ticks, mites, and harvestmen (daddy longlegs). Like insects, spiders are arthropods, and have jointed legs and segmented bodies. But spiders differ from insects in significant ways. Insects have six legs. Spiders have eight. Insects have two large compound eyes, each with many lenses and angles of view as well as two to four simple eyes that detect changes in light and shadows. Spiders have six to eight simple eyes but no compound eyes. And while some insects spin silk, spiders spin silk so thin as to be almost invisible, yet so strong that it is considered the strongest material in nature.

All spiders have venom. Only a few kinds of spiders, such as the black widow, the brown recluse spider, and the tarantula, have venom strong enough to be dangerous to people. Get medical help if you are bitten by one of these.

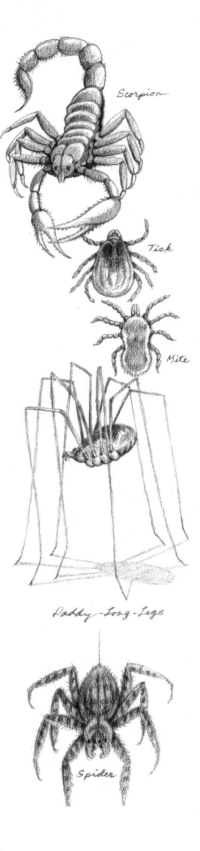

Scorpion

Tick

Mite

Daddy-Long-Legs

Spider

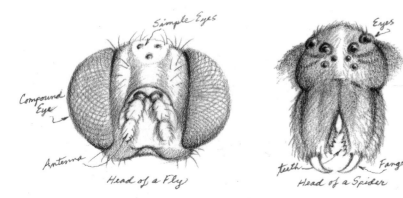

Simple Eyes

Compound Eye

Antenna

Head of a Fly

Eyes

teeth

Fangs

Head of a Spider

The brown recluse spider is sometimes called the violin spider because of the violin-shaped mark on its thorax.

The common barn spider is big but harmless. If you don't mind the presence of their large orb webs, these spiders will keep your garage free of flies.

BROWN RECLUSE SPIDER

SOUTH AMERICAN TARANTULA
(actual size)

COMMON
BARN
SPIDER

Silhouette shows average size
of North American species.

DEER TICK (known to
transmit Lyme disease)

Ticks are cousins
of spiders that
not only bite but
also suck blood.

EASTERN
WOOD
TICK

ROCKY
MOUNTAIN
WOOD TICK

merican tarantulas
, but they are the
ost tarantulas is
ul than a bee sting.
e not aggressive.

Adult Female

Adult Male

(known to transmit
Rocky Mountain spotted
fever and other diseases)

34

SUPERSIZED SPIDERS AND TICKS

Spiders use their silk to construct webs that snare prey. Depending on the species, a spiderweb can be a large oval or orb, a funnel-shaped tunnel or a zig-zag of sticky strands.

Spiders prey on insects and other small animals by paralyzing them with venom injected through sharp fangs. Any flying insect caught in a spider's web that is not eaten right away is wrapped up tightly in silk and saved for later.

At left, greatly enlarged, is a black widow spider wrapping a small moth victim. The silhouettes show the actual size of the spiders on this page. Black widow spiders are found worldwide, except in far northern latitudes. Depending on the sub-species, black widows can have a red hourglass mark on the top or on the underside of their abdomen.

There are some South whose bite can be dead exception. The bite of no more deadly or pair Tarantulas are shy and

YELLOW BUMBLEBEE AND BROOK TROUT

Mindful of the Small

One afternoon while fishing for brook trout, I spotted a large bumblebee floating helplessly downstream. How it happened to fall in the water is a mystery. But there it was, caught in the swift current. The bee drifted over small trout that rose and nipped at its wet legs. As the bee floated over a pocket of water that I knew held a fish large enough to gobble it down, I reached out, offering the tip of my fly rod. To my surprise and delight, the insect grabbed hold and held tight. Ever so slowly, I swung the rod to a streamside boulder, where the bee crawled onto the dry rock. Its yellow-and-black body was sodden. Its wings were soaked and heavy-looking and it couldn't fly. I moved as close as I could and gently blew them dry until the bee took off.

Scientists believe that insects alone make up the largest biomass on Earth. That means if we could somehow gather all of them together, their combined weight would exceed the combined weight of all the other animals. Yet unless we are getting stung or bitten or buzzed, we pay little attention to these incredibly diverse, intricately designed, and awesomely beautiful creatures.

Insects and spiders enliven the motionless ground and vibrate the invisible air, filling the world with movement and sound. They populate the space between us and the landscape. They provide a broad and bountiful foundation for the food chain. They pollinate our flowers and fertilize our crops. They add a pinch of seasoning to every outing. And perhaps most importantly, they teach us to be mindful of the small.

Author's Note

Squeezing the largest biomass on Earth into forty pages is an impossible task. My goal was much simpler—to show you some of the major orders of insects and arachnids and to tell you something interesting about each. In writing this book I learned more about the insects and spiders that I already knew and also discovered a number of fascinating new species that I had not known. As always, the methodical process of learning and the excitement of discovery made me feel even more privileged to be here on this wondrous planet.

All nature study starts with what is right in front of you—in my case, a caterpillar on the ground. This discovery led me from insect to insect, spider to spider. Most of the species you will find on these pages are fairly common around the world. For the more exotic insects or arachnids, I have listed their regions along with their names.

Not all encounters with insects or spiders are pleasant: I am often asked what to do about ticks, for example. First of all, to lessen the chance that a tick will get on me, I try to stay on mowed paths and avoid walking in brush or tall grass. These are the places ticks lurk, waiting for a host to pass. If I know I'm going to have to walk in such places, I wear a hat, long sleeves, and long pants with the cuffs tucked into my socks.

After my walk, I check my clothing and my skin for ticks. If I find a tick biting me I remove it with tweezers, taking care to remove all the embedded head and mouth parts. I visit my doctor to show the bite and describe the tick. The bite of a disease-carrying tick often shows up as a red circular rash.

No matter what, never let the possibility of an encounter with ticks or other wild creatures prevent you from enjoying the outdoors.

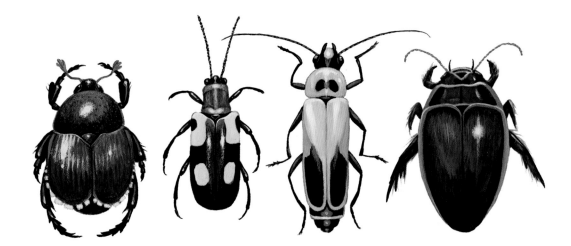

More About Insects and Spiders

Bishop, Nic. *Spiders*. New York: Scholastic, 2007.

Burns, Loree Griffin. *The Hive Detectives: Chronicle of a Honey Bee Catastrophe.* New York: Houghton Mifflin, 2010.

Davies, Hazel, and the American Museum of Natural History. *The Exquisite Butterfly Companion*. New York: Sterling, 2011.

Evans, Arthur V. *National Wildlife Federation Field Guide to Insects and Spiders of North America*. New York: Sterling, 2008.

Greenaway, Theresa. *Big Book of Bugs*. New York: Dorling Kindersley, Inc., 2000.

Lasky, Kathryn, and Christopher G. Knight. *Silk and Venom: Searching for a Dangerous Spider*. Boston: Candlewick, 2011.

Parker, Steve. *Ant Lions, Wasps & Other Insects (Animal Kingdom Classification)*. Mankato, MN: Capstone Books, 2005.

Royston, Angela. *Life Cycle of a Butterfly*, 2nd edition. Chicago: Heinemann Raintree, 2009.

Simon, Seymour. *Spiders*. New York: HarperCollins, 2008.

Tait, Noel. *Insects & Spiders (Insiders)*. New York: Simon & Schuster, 2008.

Whalley, Paul Ernest Sutton. *Butterfly & Moth (Eyewitness Guides)*. New York: Dorling Kindersley, Inc., 2000.

White, Richard E. *Beetles: A Field Guide to the Beetles of North America (Peterson Field Guides)*. New York: Houghton Mifflin, 1998.

Wilsdon, Christina. *Insects (First Field Guide, National Audubon Society)*. New York: Scholastic, 1998.

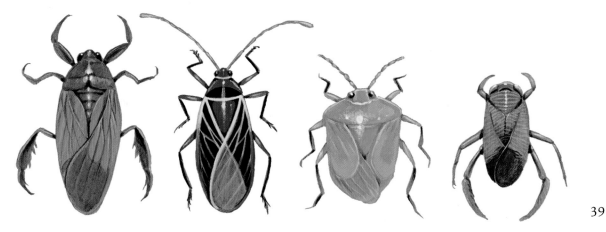

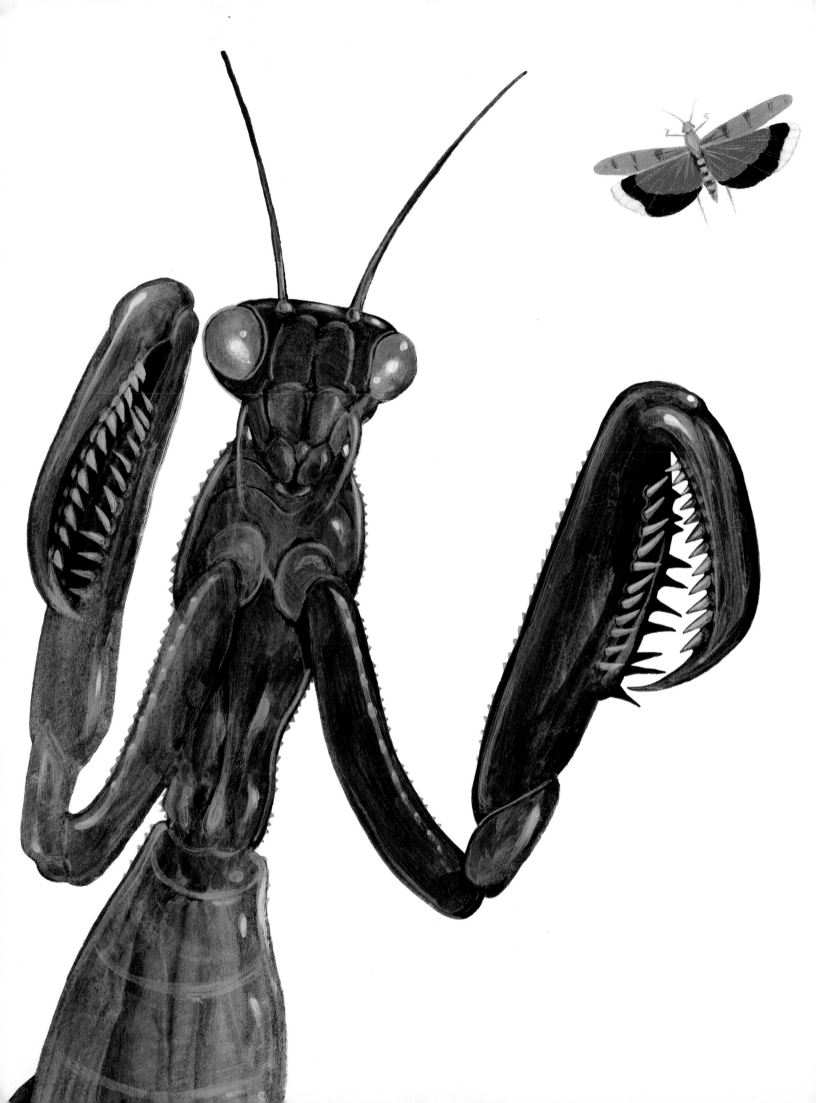